Transforming Lives

WOODBRIDGE
International
Mergers & Acquisitions Since 1993

Call 203.389.8400 or visit us at woodbridgegrp.com

Don Krier
Senior Managing Director/Partner
New Business
ext. 201
dkrier@woodbridgegrp.com

Larry Reinharz
Senior Managing Director/Partner
New Business
ext. 209
lreinharz@woodbridgegrp.com

This Book is a Quick Read

©2023 Woodbridge International
All rights reserved.
ISBN 979-8-218-25445-2

Legal Disclaimers and End User Rights

10th Book

WOODBRIDGE
International
Mergers & Acquisitions Since 1993

30 Years of Lessons Learned

Selling Middle-Market Businesses

TABLE OF CONTENTS

Introduction:
Why You Should Read This Book

Robert Koenig
Founder and CEO
Woodbridge International

WOODBRIDGE
International
Mergers & Acquisitions Since 1993

Woodbridge International
Robert Koenig

As Woodbridge International celebrates its 30th anniversary, we want to tell you our story—from our humble beginnings to where we are today—and we think you will be able to relate. Why? Because we are you. We were a startup, working from our living rooms and kitchen tables.

Like many of you, I had a family business. And when I sold it in 1993, we hired an investment banker, but they only came up with one buyer. They didn't create an auction or a competitive environment. They didn't get people competing for our business. As a result, I walked away with nothing. I didn't get anything out of the deal because they didn't get us the best deal.

At the time, we thought that was the only way to do it, because I didn't know any better. But it stuck with me and left me feeling like there was a better way. It made me realize that you've got to cast a wide net. You've got to have options.

I think a lot of people feel that there's only one logical buyer for their business. They're selling their single-largest asset, but they don't have enough information to ensure they're making the right decision.

Meanwhile, with no money and no clients, I was looking for a business to buy, and I couldn't find one. That's how I got the idea to start Woodbridge International. I figured, if I couldn't find a business to buy, then probably a lot of others couldn't either.

I saw a gap in the industry—a problem that needed solving—so I launched Woodbridge to solve it.

We started on the buy side. We cast a wide net, and it worked. And we realized, if it works on the buy side, it's going to work on the sell side too. And that's how Woodbridge International was born.

Those early days were tough. We were undercapitalized and bootstrapped, driven by grit and passion to succeed. We had never done this before and we didn't go to school for it. I don't have an MBA, but I had real-world experience running a small business, and there's no substitute for experience. We had no choice but to succeed. We had to figure it out—our families depended on it.

From scrappy entrepreneurs...

Don Krier, our Senior Managing Director, was there with me since the beginning, was driving an unregistered, uninsured vehicle. He recalls this story: "I remember sitting at a traffic light one Friday night, looking around and wondering how many people got a paycheck this week. We were waiting for a commission check to come in and it hadn't come yet. And I went home and I took everything I had in my pocket and I put it on the dresser and I realized all I had was what I just held in my hand. It was 42 cents, and I had a wife and three kids at the time. Talk about humble beginnings!"

We know firsthand the gut-wrenching feeling of having to make payroll. If there wasn't enough one week, we didn't get paid. In 1993, our first year in business, we signed three buy-side clients and got three deals done, but we didn't take a paycheck. In 1994, we took on four clients and got four deals done. In 1995, we switched to the sell side. In 1997, we developed our first website. In 2001, the dot-com crash happened, and we went an entire year without closing a deal. We had to pull in our horns, not take pay, and work our butts off. We were able to close a deal in 2002. Then we had a very good run up until 2008. In fact, we had our best year in 2007.

In 2009, after the Great Recession decimated the financial industry, we went six months without paying ourselves because our business came to a grinding halt. When times were tough, we paid our people but not ourselves. We always put the company first.

We recognize that you have gone through a lot of the same anguish we did over the years. The entrepreneurial journey is a road traveled by a select few. It tests families, relationships and, at times, the core of your very being. So we understand the blood, sweat, and tears that went into creating your business, because we've been there ourselves.

...to 30 years strong!

Here we are 30 years later. We had our best year ever in 2022! In almost every year we've been in business, we've gotten better than the year before. And now we're celebrating our 30th anniversary. Two-thirds of all businesses fail within the first 10 years—a quarter in the first year.[1] To survive and especially thrive for 30 years is a big deal.

Here's another measure of success: Senior managing director Don Krier is still with me. Senior managing director Larry Reinharz has been with me since 2005 and senior managing director and COO Marni Connelly since 2002. Today, they are all partners. Why have they stayed? Because we have built an environment with an entrepreneurial spirit that provides them with an opportunity to roll up their sleeves and play a role in molding and shaping the company. And I know for a fact I could not have done it on my own. Together, we created something from nothing. And our clients are better for it.

How did we get where we are today? To say the least, this has been both an evolution and a massive learning experience for us. And it's in the adversity where we've learned the most. We have grown from a two-person firm to a 90-person firm through trial and error, successes, and failures.

And you learn more in the tough times than in the good times. In the startup period, in the dot-com crash, in the Great Recession— the lessons we learned were that you have to work harder to work smarter, act with a sense of urgency to make decisions, be decisive, and avoid being paralyzed. And you have to monitor the decisions, and if they're wrong immediately fix them and change them, but have a plan and stick to the plan.

Our core business is unique and it's been developed over the years playing the odds. It's a numbers game. And what we've learned is, we're on the right track. But use those things that derail you to learn.

Put yourself in a position where you have to figure it out, where your back is to the wall and it's a matter of survival. When you go into survival mode, you can do amazing things. Every business owner goes through a journey; this is our journey—filled with 30 years of experiences and lessons learned. We trust that as you read this book, you will see yourself in many of our stories. And we hope, after reading it, that you come away with tremendous insight from our experiences that you can use in your own business.

As you turn the page to read more about our lessons learned, keep these three 'golden rules of business' in mind:

- Surround yourself with people who are better than you at what they do

- Play by the numbers—track and measure everything you do

- Be learning-centric, and continually improve, evolve, change, and adapt

In addition, every chapter has three key "Lessons Learned" at the end. We hope that the lessons we impart in these chapters help to make you and your business even more successful; and should you decide to sell, these lessons can help you with that decision as well.

WOODBRIDGE
International

1764 Litchfield Turnpike | Suite 250 | New Haven, CT 06525
203.389.8400 | woodbridgegrp.com

“ Culture is king. We have found, without a doubt, that integration of culture beats strategy and breeds success. **”**

Kyle Richard
Managing Partner, Closing
Woodbridge International

WOODBRIDGE
International
Mergers & Acquisitions Since 1993

Chapter 1

BUILD A COLLABORATIVE TEAM CULTURE

What exactly is culture in a company environment? Your business's culture is everyone having a positive attitude and a strong work ethic. It's being aligned and on the same page about your *why* and *how*. It's functioning as a team for the greater good, and not worrying about receiving individual credit. It's a constant flow of communication that keeps the company running smoothly on a day-to-day basis, focuses everyone on solutions instead of problems, and always keeps an eye toward setting and/or maximizing future trends.

Why should having a positive company culture be important to you? Having a healthy, cohesive culture can give your company a leg up. The firms we take to market that have a great culture, buyers feel it. The firms we take to market that have a poor culture, buyers feel that too. When a potential buyer sees a company with a great culture, they see a well-oiled machine they can feel confident will continue running smoothly after the takeover. Should you decide to sell, this could help you attract both higher bids and companies that are a better fit.

Our culture here at Woodbridge developed organically. We didn't force it. And it took several years to become what it is today. Perhaps knowing how we developed our culture over time can help you understand how to further develop yours.

Lesson 1: Always maintain control of your business

In the beginning, Woodbridge used an affiliate program to reach global buyers and sellers. Sales were conducted through 21 partner offices worldwide. After some time, it became clear that we didn't have as much control over the deals as we wanted and there was no cohesive culture. Everyone did things their own way to a degree, and some deals took forever to close, or never closed. Our close rate was less than 50 percent. Today, it's close to 80 percent.

After a few years, it was determined that the affiliate program wasn't working to our advantage. "Our deal closers were independent contractors, so they had the freedom to do other things," recalls Reinharz. "Our thinking was, if they don't close, they're not going to make money. But they started operating out of fear; they weren't getting tough with buyers, and they weren't listening to us or taking direction."

When someone is on salary, they're going to listen to you and take direction. The affiliates had their own methodology that was slightly different from everyone else, so the team wasn't always in sync. After eight years, we discontinued the affiliate program and hired in-house employees, and that's when Woodbridge's positive, collaborative culture began to take shape. But simply hiring staff wasn't, by itself, enough to foster a healthy culture. There was one additional change we needed to make.

Lesson 2: Hire trainable employees

At first, we hired seasoned deal closers who were experienced in the industry, but they didn't assimilate well into the Woodbridge environment. They thought they knew better than everyone else, and no one worked together. They didn't have the same values, and deals weren't getting done. It was a very siloed feeling throughout the firm, and the company struggled significantly with that.

A traditional investment banking firm has older employees who are used to doing things a certain way. But Woodbridge is anything but traditional. With my background as an entrepreneur, I wanted to do things a little differently, and better.

So we pivoted a second time and hired younger employees we could train and mold in the Woodbridge way of doing things. They didn't necessarily have an investment banking background. There was no guarantee it would work, and many people were skeptical at the time; but it did work—really well in fact—because everyone became aligned culturally, and the benefits have been measurable.

"Nobody is there to just ride the train," says Partner Simon Wibberley. "Everyone contributes, and we're not afraid to fail." A diversity of backgrounds combined with open-mindedness and common goals and interests drives great ideas, he says. "If you make a suggestion and it doesn't work, your job isn't on the line. We analyze why something didn't work and learn from our mistakes."

I'm also passionate about promoting from within to grow people up through the company, so there's tremendous opportunity here for team members to both use their own voice and take on additional responsibility over time.

But we don't have novices working on deals. The partners are the ones with the experience and the tribal knowledge we've gained over the years. They are mentoring, coaching, and training the staff to do things the way we've learned is best for the client. With every single deal, the partners know what's going on. We're debating what's next, how to negotiate each deal better, and how to find a buyer with certainty to close, not just with the highest price. We're the ones with the knowledge and control, and they learned it from us. That's a crucial point.

Here's what cultural alignment looks like at Woodbridge: Now that we're one firm working together, nobody passes the blame. And in the daily partner meetings, there's a common goal. If something doesn't work, everyone takes ownership. When we promoted from within, that's when we really started to see that change for the better.

We've been operating this new model of home-grown, home-trained staff since 2017. Over six years, the evolution has been significant, to the point where we had our best year ever in 2022. Now we're at a new plateau and the bar has been set very high.

Lesson 3: Take a best-of-breed approach

In the traditional investment banking model, one person does everything from start to finish—signing up the client, writing the book, doing the research, sending out the mailing, talking to all the parties, negotiating the deal, and closing it.

At Woodbridge, the M&A process is divided into specialties. So instead of one person handling your entire sale from A to Z, each person handles one function, and has a broader scope of understanding of their own specialty. A professional business writer writes your book. A professional accountant looks at your books and numbers. A professional closer negotiates your deal and closing.

Our team is specialized and focused, and it allows us to customize the work to fit the specific needs of the client. We've learned over time that we get more deals done faster because each person is an expert in his or her specialty.

Lesson 4: Stay connected

Although our environment is global, it's very collaborative and connected. In addition to the U.S., we've got employees in South Africa, but it feels like they're in the office next to me because we're all connected and in sync—everyone checks in with their team throughout the day.

When you run a global operation, it's a challenge to get people on separate continents to feel like they're part of the same organization. To keep everything running smoothly, team collaboration is key. And the constant communication helps our clients see better success.

Also, a collaborative, connected environment provides better problem-solving. With programs like Zoom and DealRoom—our project management software—the full team gets to hear about issues that may be bubbling up on another engagement that they're not directly involved with. They can weigh in, add value to the situation, learn from it, and then apply what they've learned to their own experiences. This creates better problem-solving, while also fostering a learning environment.

Key Lessons Learned:

- *Hire trainable people who are team-oriented and have a can-do attitude*

- *Maintain control of your processes at the leadership level to influence a positive culture*

- *Nurture a solution-oriented, problem-solving environment*

WOODBRIDGE
International

1764 Litchfield Turnpike | Suite 250 | New Haven, CT 06525
203.389.8400 | woodbridgegrp.com

❝ We've made a lot of mistakes, but we don't repeat them. That has made us what we are. **❞**

Robert Koenig
Founder
Woodbridge International

Chapter 2

TAKE RISKS; BREAK NEW MARKETING GROUND; DON'T BE AFRAID TO FAIL

How often do you try new marketing techniques? Do your marketing efforts help your company rise above the clutter? Or are you just playing it safe and doing what everyone else in your industry does? Taking marketing risks can help your company realize its growth potential. And growth potential is one of the key factors potential buyers look for in a company to buy.

We've been taking marketing risks to find both buyers and sellers since Woodbridge opened its doors, and many of these techniques—from being an early adopter of Internet advertising to writing, printing, and mailing hard-copy books, distributing them to our entire database, and using videos to provide buyers with an inside look at sellers' companies—have been highly effective.

We also have continually increased our budget. New business spend has increased approximately 65 percent over the last two years, and the benefit has been evident. We had the best years of our 30-year history in 2021 and 2022!

When my son Jacob was in high school, he would spend his summers at the office burning CDs of client videos and mailing them to potential buyers. At the time, it was new technology, but that personal touch allowed potential buyers to see inside a company and get to know the management to a degree. Internet videos didn't exist yet, so we were well ahead of the curve.

"We started buying keywords on the Internet in 2000 and it generated a lot of leads," recalls Reinharz, but we didn't convert our first lead until 2004. It took us four years to figure out how to sift through companies that weren't qualified and find the high-value leads. "At the time, there were no other M&A firms doing business that way, so we were ahead of that curve. Also, the market continually evolves, and we still continue to evolve along with it, while some other firms have tried and failed.

There's no crystal ball to what works and what doesn't. We've tried different things at different times. Some ideas worked; some didn't. We certainly didn't know the things we tried were going to work. We just tested them and measured our efforts. However, over the years, having people dedicated to online marketing and having enough volume for lead generation has helped.

"The same thing happened with our website," Krier recalls. "One time, we reconfigured it, and our leads dropped by 50 percent overnight. We had to go back to an older format that was giving us better performance. We took a big risk and it didn't work, but because we tracked our results (leads, conversions, webinar attendees, etc.), we knew within a week that it wasn't going to work and we were able to act quickly."

Lesson 5: Cast a wide net

One of our most successful marketing risks was the launch of our global auction process. Most investment banking firms, when representing a company's sale, approach 20 to 200 of the 'most likely' buyers, which generates two or three bids.

Woodbridge casts a wider net for potential buyers than traditional investment bankers do, approaching anywhere from 8,000 to 15,000 customized buyers. The net result is, sellers get seen by many more organizations, and often are bought by companies in industries they might not have realized are a good fit.

Today, our database contains over 1 million records, and it's taken 30 years to build the database we have. But we're constantly refreshing and developing it. When our database was small but growing, we didn't have anywhere near this type of success.

For each client, we make about 15,000 contacts to talk to 100 to 500 people who are interested. We reach the same potential buyers our competitors would, as well as thousands more. But because of the size of our database, "If a sale doesn't work and we have to re-market a company, 90 percent of the interested buyers we send out to the second time are new," says Reinharz. "So that's big, because people want to know, what's my risk? And we can say, if it doesn't happen the first time out, it's okay, because we've got a solution. We're empowering the business owner and seller, instead of doing things on the buyer's schedule and sucking up to them. That's how we do it."

It's a numbers game, and to a degree it's counterintuitive to go to a wide audience because most companies want their sale kept confidential. They don't want their employees, competitors or vendors to know. But confidentiality is not an issue with us because of the way we do it. Also, it used to cost thousands of dollars to mail a blind executive summary, but now we use email. The cost is significantly lower and they receive it instantly. This is another way we've evolved.

Lesson 6: Educate, don't sell

In 2015, we published a book to help business owners understand the selling process and better prepare them for selling their business. We started with a book called *How to Sell Your Midsize Business*. It was written by one of our affiliates and downloadable from our website.

In 2018, we started writing our own books. The first time we tried it, we didn't have a lot of excess cash flow. We mailed it out to prospects and they loved it. We didn't know it would work, but we did know owners were looking to be educated. And they loved the content, so we thought, why not blanket our target market? It was a big financial risk, but it paid off, and it really has been a game changer for us.

The book you are reading right now is our 10th book. Each one is distributed to our entire 230,000 database of business owners all over the U.S. and Canada. We have distributed more than 2 million printed, hard copies of books since the inception of this marketing program.

Today, we do about three book mailings a year to help educate our target market. Now clients are viewing us in a whole different way from others, and this has become one of our points of differentiation—our niche and our angle —and it gets us better clients.

Kyle Richard recalls when the company tried switching to postcards to save money. "We discovered that it wasn't educating anybody on anything. Postcards were just beating our own chest in the market, and we never got a bump in new business from it," he says. "The postcards didn't work because they were too self-serving and not educational."

Remember, I'm a mid-market business owner and a marketing-minded entrepreneur, not a traditional investment banker. Because of that, my background has helped us develop more novel and innovative ways to market privately held companies for sale. Also, everyone on the team comes from different sides of the business with different backgrounds. That makes us unique, because we're not using grandfathered ideology about how things should work. These varied people bring different ideas and opinions to the table for consideration, and that helps us to think differently as a team. Diversity of backgrounds is our strength.

What different backgrounds do you and your team have and how can you use that to your advantage when coming up with marketing ideas? If you're using ideas that others in your industry use and they work for you, great. But you won't stand out in the crowd that way. Look for ideas that break boundaries and barriers. If something doesn't work, stop. If it works, incrementally grow your efforts. Whatever you do, keep moving forward!

Lesson 7: Embrace failure and learn from it

We have failed—dozens of times. But the lessons we've learned from those failures have pointed us in better, more profitable directions. Consider, for example, the affiliate program mentioned in Chapter 1. That's a great example of an idea that didn't work, but we wouldn't be where we are today if we hadn't seen the view from the other side and gone through that process.

Another idea the firm undertook that did not pay off was selling international companies. "We always marketed businesses globally," recalls Reinharz. "In 2011, we started selling businesses overseas. We began with direct marketing in Brazil and I went to Brazil several times. Then we started doing the same thing in India and all over Europe."

Woodbridge was good at getting clients, and that wave of success lasted for three or four years. But what we learned is that the U.S. is still the best place in the world to do business. Buyers globally wanted businesses in the U.S. and Canada. They didn't necessarily want to buy in Latin America, India or even Europe, although companies in Latin America, India, and Europe wanted to buy businesses here. And that is still true today.

There's so much innovation happening today that if something isn't working for you, there are plenty more ideas to choose from. So never live with the status quo, even if you think the status quo is working. It will make you stagnant and stunt your growth.

Always explore new ways to market your services and become more efficient.

Right now, the newest idea is how you can use artificial intelligence (AI) in your company. We're exploring that here at Woodbridge International and we strongly suggest every business explore AI to see how it can help what they're doing, because ultimately it's going to help.

Lesson 8: Step outside your comfort zone

If you take a risk and you're not scared, and it feels comfortable, then you're probably not taking a big enough risk. Risk should scare the hell out of you, but you do it anyway because the idea has merit and you know that some risk is necessary in business.

It's the tribal knowledge, the mistakes, and the lessons learned that build your gut instinct and your intuition. So believe in yourselves. You trust your gut and you draw on the years of knowledge, wisdom, and experience you've gained. Then as your gut gets better, you connect the dots faster. That's why we had two of our best years in '21 and '22. We trust our gut; we know how to capitalize on an idea, and we know what to do. That's why our clients trust us.

Here's a good example. Five years ago, Woodbridge opened an office in Cape Town, South Africa. We had never opened a branch office in another country before. This was a big risk, but the robust talent pool and the strong work ethic of the potential employees fit well with our unique business model. So we decided to take the plunge. We started out small, with just a few employees in two departments.

"When we began, we just handled business development," says Wibberley, a partner who manages the Cape Town office. "We had three people initially doing more administrative tasks who never worked in M&A before. And they were getting it done. We were achieving results and it was generating a lot of interest for us."

Our headquarters, however, is in the United States. We are an American company and always will be. We don't take on clients in South Africa. As we said, there's no market like the United States and Canada. But our Cape Town employees help us serve our North American clients.

Today, in Cape Town, we have 65 employees who work across every department, and we think it's one of the best moves we ever made. The talent we have there is world-class and provides tremendous value. Wibberley calls it one of the best examples of "what you put in is what you get out," saying its contribution to Woodbridge has made the company "leaner, slicker, faster, and more profitable"…all to the benefit of our clients.

Key Lessons Learned:

- Trust your gut

- Don't be afraid to take risks in how you market your company

- Start small but continually test and invest in your growth

" There's so much innovation happening today. If something isn't working for you, there's plenty more to choose from. "

Simon Wibberley, Partner
Managing Director
Cape Town Operations

WOODBRIDGE
International
Mergers & Acquisitions Since 1993

Chapter 3

RECOGNIZE 'AHA MOMENTS' AS OPPORTUNITIES

Many of the lessons learned that we share in this book came as the result of an 'aha moment'. Aha moments happen when you see an opportunity to fill a gap or solve a problem for yourself or your customers before anyone else does.

For example, when I first started Woodbridge International in 1993, we represented buyers, not sellers. We would sign buyers on as clients and then go out to companies that were a good fit and say, 'We've got a buyer interested in a business like yours. Would you be interested in selling?'

Lesson 9: Always be ready to pivot

After about three years, however, we realized we were better able to serve our market while also growing our company by representing the seller. So we changed our model in 1996 to focus on where we saw the opportunity to cast a wide net and play the numbers game, which we were good at. That was an aha moment in and of itself. But another quickly followed.

Krier recalls: "When we first started representing sellers, we thought, you put a buyer and seller together and walk away and the deal would just close. I remember one year we literally had 70 or 80 sales on the board, and none of them happened. What we learned is that we were not involved enough. We couldn't just leave them to their own devices; we had to get involved."

The aha moment was that we have to be in the middle. "We have to keep the sale process moving," says Krier. "We have to make sure buyers' questions get answered. When we realized that, we were able to monitor and control the flow and type of information that would pass between the buyer and the seller and make sure it happened at the appropriate pace and time."

We had a client that stopped the process twice and took his company off the market because he was scared. So we spent time talking with him about this. He ultimately came around; the business was sold and he stayed on with the company for about a year after the sale.

One of the things we realized was that a seller needs to be able to identify what they're going to do post sale. What do they want life to look like? This is one area where we got involved—asking whether they were prepared for the sale emotionally and mentally and whether they had a plan. We saw that we needed to facilitate this conversation to help them develop an honest assessment of their feelings and to help them prepare on a personal level for the transition. Once we got involved in this and ensured sellers were ready when the company went out to bid, it helped get deals done faster.

Have you ever had a client tell you about a problem requiring a solution that was not in your current wheelhouse, and you walked away wondering how you could solve the problem for them? When you come up with that solution, that's an aha moment. Especially if that idea results in a new line of business for you. Also, solving problems is a high-value trait to have. Being solution-focused and forward-thinking is something buyers look for in a potential business acquisition.

Lesson 10: Help customers help themselves

One of Woodbridge's biggest aha moments came six years ago when we realized the need for a management training program to teach sellers how to think like buyers.

We discovered that business owners had no experience in how to sell their business; they didn't know what to say or how to say it, or they were saying the wrong things, and they weren't being coached in how to say the right things. So we developed a program to help them prepare for their meetings with potential buyers, and what they learn in the program can often lead to owners uncovering some of their own unique aha moments about their business.

For example, many owners don't want to inform their key people of the fact that they're selling because they fear the unknown. However, all of our clients who did tell their key people had a positive outcome. Their key people appreciated it and understood that they would be crucial to the buyer.

Also, we discovered early on that many sellers didn't know how to behave in a management meeting with potential buyers. Professor Andy Gole, who teaches the two-day course for us, knew owners liked to process issues with non-competing leaders from other industries with similar challenges, so he suggested we bring sellers together to bond and learn from each other.

The biggest challenge was helping sellers understand how to think from the buyer's perspective. Consider a manufacturing company with an expensive machine. The replacement cost is $1 million. The manufacturer's recommended useful life is 15 years. The machine is now in its 20th year and still humming like a top. There's nothing wrong with it. A seller is going to say, "This machine is great, no problem." But the buyer is going to say, "I have to put money aside to buy a new machine," and will probably want to reduce the selling price by $1 million.

In this situation, sellers would make the strongest case possible for the machine's longevity, perhaps providing maintenance records. But there's no denying the rated machine life, so we would prepare the seller for a realistic concession.

Since its inception, the management training program has constantly evolved. In the beginning, the two-day session was 60 days into the timeline. We learned, however, that this was too late, because the creative team had already completed the video and confidential information memorandum (CIM), and the training drew out deep insights we needed to include in the marketing materials. So we adjusted the schedule to put the training at the beginning. This was an aha moment.

Key Lessons Learned:

- *Recognize aha moments as opportunities for new ideas*

- *Find solutions to customer problems that no one else is solving, or that you can solve better*

- *Be ready to pivot when things don't go as planned or when new opportunities are uncovered along the way*

WOODBRIDGE
International

1764 Litchfield Turnpike | Suite 250 | New Haven, CT 06525
203.389.8400 | woodbridgegrp.com

ff Every time we think we're
starting to level off, we find
something else that continues
to differentiate us and make
us unique. **JJ**

Marni Connelly, Partner
Senior Managing Director
and Chief Operating Officer
Woodbridge International

WOODBRIDGE
International
Mergers & Acquisitions Since 1993

Chapter 4

USE TECH TO STAY INNOVATIVE AND FORWARD-THINKING

Overall, I think our success has come from always feeling like a startup, always feeling like we've never really made it, always feeling like we've got to drive the business, and never resting on our laurels. But technology has helped us achieve all that.

Every day, it helps us devise forward-thinking marketing ideas, build on our successes, challenge people to make their jobs exciting and not mundane, align everyone around common problems, experiences, and goals, collaborate and communicate, automate redundant tasks, improve processes, measure progress and success, and learn from our mistakes.

Salesforce, for example, helps the Woodbridge team manage potential sales and customer accounts. But we didn't always have such a useful tool. "In the early days, I had a thousand sheets of paper on my desk—one for every company I called," recalls Krier. "And I was making hand-written notes on every one of them. When desktop computers became available, we adapted immediately to digitize and keep track of all our data in ACT."

Krier recalls the days when his five kids would sit around the dining room table and stuff envelopes. "That was our mailing house," he says. "We would print letters, I would sign them, somebody else would fold them and stuff them in the envelopes, and someone else would seal them and put stamps on them. It's become much more sophisticated now because the company keeps adapting and evolving. Systems have improved; and our technology has advanced with the times and streamlined our business. We can do more with fewer people better and faster."

Woodbridge also was early to use e-signing for nondisclosure agreements (NDAs). Signing NDAs is a two-week process for many investment banking firms. For us, from the time someone gets a teaser to when they sign an NDA and get a CIM, our process moves much faster than the industry norm. And our buyers often sign quickly, because of all the information we provide to them in the CIM. So that helps keep the momentum of the deal going, because time kills all deals.

Lesson 11: Let data feed your decisions

With technology comes valuable data. For example, the reporting and the key performance indicators we get from Salesforce help to provide clarity, so everyone knows whether a particular project is meeting its goals. I think that has helped make us successful.

Our database is the catalyst that has given very quick results to our clients because we're able to reach a significant amount of buyers within hours. "Sometimes we get an immediate response from potential buyers," says Partner Kyle Richard. "For a lot of our competitors, that process can take weeks, months, sometimes even years to get the education that we get very, very quickly."

Our auction process is the opposite of that. We're moving things fast. For us, there's a sense of urgency and getting things done quickly. And we're doing things in parallel instead of in a series. It would be hard to do that if things were moving slow. This is just one example of how we're using technology and innovation to put our clients in the best position to succeed.

Lesson 12: Streamline and automate all you can

Woodbridge continually looks for opportunities to standardize and formalize practices and processes at each step of the deal, including bid forms, email automation, client onboarding, financial underwriting, writing the CIMs, and e-signing NDAs. These process improvements have shortened both our time from marketing launch to close and our time from engagement to close.

By streamlining and automating processes, team members are able to manage two to three times more workflow than if they were in an in-person setting, but it's getting done more efficiently, thanks to technology. Also, automating repetitive tasks frees up staff for focusing their time on strategic thinking and idea generation to promote problem-solving and business growth.

Achieving these goals means continually investing in technology, such as Salesforce, Egnyte, DealRoom, Constant Contact, Foxit, eSign and more. Everything we do is to make a better experience for our clients. And when we realize that what we did helped us and helped our clients, then we make the decision to keep going in that direction or pivot to something else.

For instance, bids were up 15 percent from 2021 to 2022 and they are projected to rise another 15 percent this year. And the number of campaigns with 25 or more bids is also projected to increase 20 percent this year! Also, the more bids we get, the more likely the deal is to close. As the number of bids go up past 20 and toward 40, our success rate significantly increases. More qualified leads means more buyers, more bids, a higher price, and a better fit for every client and every sale.

"In the long run, anything a computer does better than a person, eventually the computer will be doing, so automate what's automatable and leave the personal high-touch actions to humans," says Jacob Koenig.

Lesson 13: Look for simple technology with a huge ROI

A perfect example of automation with value is when everyone had to pivot from doing business in-person to running their businesses remotely.

"Normally," recalls Reinharz, "we would get on a plane and visit potential clients, and we'd also bring them to our office. But in 2008, when the Great Recession stalled the financial and other industries, we started setting up video conferences and cut back on traveling to business owners' offices. Plus, there was a tremendous benefit because we could patch in our whole team instead of a meeting just being one-on-one. So now it's not just about me, it's about the entire organization."

Fast forward to March, 2020. By the time the pandemic caused a nationwide shutdown, Zoom was already in wide use across Woodbridge, and it quickly gave the firm a competitive edge. We flipped the company into the digital space in 48 hours, because 80 percent of the required functionality was already in place. All we had to do was a little bit of education to get everyone up to speed on the platform, and it quickly turned our company into a digital environment.

Not every business was that lucky. "For all of us in the investment banking industry, when COVID happened, our pipeline dried up," recalls Michael Carter, Managing Partner of investment banking firm Carter Morse & Goodrich—both a Woodbridge colleague and competitor. "People were pulling sales off the market, and the market was frozen. That was potentially life threatening. A lot of firms either had to close up, lay people off, or really hunker down. But not Woodbridge. They kept deals moving."

Now, video conferencing technology is embedded in the Woodbridge company culture. It keeps staff informed, engaged, and on the same page, no matter where they are or what time zone they're in. Consider Priscilla Schmieder, vice president of marketing communications and underwriting. She's located in Brazil, but manages a team in South Africa. Zoom facilitates that well. "Before Zoom, when I had to be on a microphone in the middle of the conference table, everyone in South Africa was in one room and they could see each other, but I couldn't see them," she recalls. "It's different now. Zoom technology puts everyone on equal footing."

Carter gives Robert Koenig credit for not only getting through the pandemic, but being confident that Woodbridge was going to survive and planning for the record years they had in '21 and '22. "That didn't happen by accident," says Carter. "A lot of people didn't have record years, and Woodbridge did. They were able to handle the crisis, and that's how you can tell how good a firm is— by how they handle a crisis, not by how they handle success."

Lesson 14: Always keep an eye on future tech

I think ChatGPT, or artificial intelligence (AI) in general, can make us better. Like us, it keeps evolving and learning, and that can be beneficial to us. I think it could possibly be a game changer in the future for us as well as others. As disruptive technology, we have to learn to work with it and adopt it, as we've done with all the technology we've brought on. Technology is not what makes us what we are and it's not what makes your business what it is. We would be successful without it. Technology supports our strategies and streamlines our tactics.

But just like in the early 2000s when we were using pay-per-click online advertising before anyone else, it's important to always keep on top of what's out there and to test new tech to see how it can both fit into and help grow your business.

Key Lessons Learned:

- *Invest in technology that automates redundant processes and improves your capabilities*

- *Step out of your comfort zone and test new tech early; continually measure results to find the ones that drive efficiency, effectiveness, and increased sales*

- *When you make technology decisions ask yourself, how can this help us improve our customers' experience?*

WOODBRIDGE
International

1764 Litchfield Turnpike | Suite 250 | New Haven, CT 06525
203.389.8400 | woodbridgegrp.com

" As the owner-operator, you're not going to be there long term. So don't talk about how great you are; talk about how well the company can run without you. "

Jacob Koenig
Partner
Deal Execution
Woodbridge International

WOODBRIDGE
International
Mergers & Acquisitions Since 1993

Chapter 5

THINK LIKE A BUYER

Should you decide to sell, there's a tremendous amount of planning and forethought that goes into it. Most business owners understand the bulk of what needs to be done. But there's one thing we can help with that most sellers often don't understand, and that's thinking like the buyer. The best way to attract the right buyer for your company is to think from the buyer's perspective. It's about the way you pitch your company to a buyer. It's not by saying, 'I'm great, look at what I've built.'

A buyer will want to be satisfied that the company can run successfully without you once you leave. So it's important to show potential buyers you have a solid team in place. We realized early on that focusing on the owner would be counterproductive. Instead, we learned over time how to help owners put together a team that potential buyers could trust.

Lesson 15: Put the best leadership team together

To maximize selling price, business owners will sometimes change their leadership team a year or six months prior to selling the business.

We had one company where the owner was stepping down and there was nobody qualified to run the business. They hired a new CEO from a competitor, and brought him to the management meeting. In the end, the seller felt bringing the new CEO to the management meeting was the single-most important reason he got top dollar forhis business—he showed buyers who was going to run the business.

Lesson 16: Prepare your executive team for the sale

Often, owners try to keep the potential sale a secret from management so as not to negatively affect morale or cause top talent to leave. Most sellers begin Woodbridge's two-day management training program thinking they're going to do the presenting and handle the Q&A by themselves. But that would not benefit the sale.

Prospective buyers are going to want to meet the executive team, and finding the right buyer has a lot to do with who you bring to the meeting with you. Here's why. The buyer won't accept your word that you have a great, cohesive, coachable team who can take over after you are gone. The buyer generally will want to meet key players, including the CEO, President, CFO, and head of sales, to name a few. Ideally, where you have strong relationships with your senior team, it's important to let them know you are planning a sale prior to the auction and to bring them to meetings with prospective buyers.

Lesson 17: Put your financials in order

Weak financial records is one of the biggest things that slows down the ability to get a company to market. Make sure you've got a great CFO, controller, and accounting firm. Don't try to minimize your expenditure on your accounting fees. Spend what you need to ensure your house is in order so you can stand behind your financials. That's absolutely critical.

Also, watch out for surprises in closings—legal, financial, and employee surprises—they're always there. Mentally prepare yourself. It also helps to have a good advisor to help you walk through crisis situations in these transactions.

Years ago we were selling a machine shop. There was a three-month delay in getting the company to market because their financials weren't in order. We got under contract with a strong buyer for $12 million and the deal was scheduled to close in 60 days. But weeks into the due diligence, our client lost his major customer and it negatively impacted his profitability and economics. So the deal had to wait. When he replaced his customer and got back on track, we brought it back to market, but in this case, his hands were tied. He was personally leveraged and needed to get out of his personal guarantee. We did end up closing the deal with a buyer for a payout over time; however, he received minimal cash at closing after a three-month delay, which cost him 60 percent of his liquidity.

Lesson 18: Prepare a unique, exciting 'future' story

Your future story—how successful the company might be after it's sold—is the most important part of the sale process, because it shows potential new owners the possibilities of where they can take the company to generate growth. This is a key area of concentration in our two-day management training session. Here's why.

Sellers generally prefer to tell a conservative future story to avoid promising a result they can't guarantee. This is understandable—from the seller's perspective. But being conservative could eliminate many buyers who are seeking businesses with greater growth potential.

We advise that when prepping your future story, business owners should realistically include all the secondary projects you considered over the years but never implemented. You want to eliminate skepticism on the part of the buyer. Skeptical buyers will protect themselves by deferring part of the sale price to future earnouts.

Contrarily, having a really strong future story creates FOMO—fear of missing out—among buyers. It causes them to sign an NDA, submit a strong non-binding bid to get into a management meeting, and submit a strong letter of intent.

Identify new market-expanding and product-increasing efficiencies and new systems, along with capital requirements and projected revenue and EBITDA. Note that anything that costs money to grow the business is less important than something that does not cost money. If it costs money, it is less attractive to a buyer. Something that doesn't cost money produces a higher return. It's all about the return on investment.

A seller with unrealistic expectations can cause a deal to blow up, however. So helping the seller understand the buyer's perspective is essential prior to meeting with potential buyers.

Lesson 19: Let your M&A partner lead

I can't tell you how many times I've spoken with a potential client who wants to sell, and they've said, 'I've been talking to this buyer for eight months now and it's not happening, and I'm really kicking myself because I shared too much information with them'. They get too specific because they don't know what to say and what not to say. We do.

Sellers often think there is a trust relationship with a potential buyer when there isn't. So you have to know what is too much information and when to share information in the process. Those are the kinds of lessons we've learned where our experience and knowledge comes into play. It protects our clients and the future of their company.

Lesson 20: Be confident about your decision to sell

Once you have decided to sell, don't question it. Don't ignore market trends, be aware of them. If your business is performing, good businesses are always in demand. And don't let macroeconomic conditions drive your motivation, your process, and your decision-making.

How do you know when it is the right time to sell? When you're mentally ready to sell your business, do it. Don't hesitate because you think interest rates are high, multiples are low, the industry is down or because other people are saying it's not the right time. Do it at the time you think makes sense and when your business is doing well. If someone says it's not a good time to sell, don't listen, because it's just not true.

Also, if the macroeconomic conditions are soft and the 'herd' mentality is it's not the right time to sell, there will be a supply-and-demand issue, just like right now with the housing market. The lack of supply means that houses are selling at a high price. It's the same for business. If there aren't enough businesses out there, you're going to stand out and get top dollar.

"Interest rates play some part in our business, but, in our section of the market, we have a lot of private equity groups that have cash to deploy," says Jacob Koenig. "So the economy is actually a much smaller factor than people may think."

It's all about how your company is performing. If sales and profits are declining, you're not going to maximize value. You need to have an upward trend. For companies that are performing and have attractive prospects, there's always market and buyer demand. As long as there is money available to lend and liquidity in the market, transactions will happen.

Lesson 21: Be emotionally and mentally prepared to sell

Ask yourself:

- How do you feel about the sale?

- Have you resolved emotionally that this is the thing to do?

- What is it you want the sale to resolve? Are you looking to retire? If so, how will your transition play out?

- Is it to recapitalize the business stronger? If so, how do you see your role? Will you stay involved but cut back on your time? What kind of equity deal are you looking for?

- How would you describe an ideal buyer? What do they bring to the table besides money?

Lesson 22: Take 'can't' out of your vocabulary

One of our biggest successes was being able to sign up a client without meeting them. Years ago, when we first started, we had a client that hired us to work for him on the buy side. He didn't have a job. He went from making $800,000 a year to not having a job and his future was dependent on us and what we were doing. He would come and sit in our office and listen to us all day.

Krier recalls, "One day, he's sitting there, and I'm on the phone talking to this potential seller, and I got him to fax his financials over to me while we were on the phone. And this gentleman was floored. He asked, 'How did you get this guy to reveal his financials and fax them to you? He didn't know you from a hole in the wall.' And I said, 'Nobody said I couldn't.'"

At Woodbridge, we approach everything as I *can*, and I *will*. That has been the mantra of how we have done things, especially when it comes to taking risks and doing new, possibly untried things. We go in with the attitude that 'we *can*'. Sometimes you learn you *can't* and you move on. When we started doing pay-per-click advertising online, using video, and offering a management training program, no one told us we couldn't. And as a result, we found out we could.

In early December 2022, I sent an article to the partners that said that, in 2022, M&A is down 35 percent from last year, and next year doesn't look good. Don Krier sent me an email that said, 'Isn't it great to have increasing market share in a down market'?

No matter the market, there are thousands of deals still taking place. We did 32 deals in 2022. And 2023 will be equally as strong.

When you're ready to sell, don't think about what you *can't* do, let us show you what you *can* do.

Key Lessons Learned:

- *Ensure that you have the right team in place*

- *Think like the buyer to help you anticipate and have answers for their questions*

- *Review and update your financials before you go to market*

WOODBRIDGE
International

ff It's nice to hear a client say,
'I never would have thought this
buyer would be such a good fit
for my company, but they are.'
And that happens time and
time again with our approach. **"**

Marni Connelly, Partner
Senior Managing Director
and Chief Operating Officer
Woodbridge International

WOODBRIDGE
International
Mergers & Acquisitions Since 1993

Chapter 6

LET US HELP YOU CHOOSE
THE RIGHT BUYER FOR YOUR COMPANY

Anyone can try and sell your business, but not all will succeed. And of those who might succeed, not all will find the best fit or get you the best deal. Over our 30 years in business, Woodbridge International has developed and honed unique processes that can make your business stand above the clutter and get it noticed by and sold to not just any buyer, but the right buyer. Here's how.

Lesson 23: Think outside the box

Most investment banking firms will have a handful of predetermined companies that they think your sale is a good fit for, and will reach out to just those firms. If all goes well, you may get two or three companies interested in buying your firm.

Many sellers come to the table saying, 'I know my business, I know my industry, who's going to buy me? It's going to be either A, B, C or D. And then all of a sudden, E comes along and the client thinks, wow, I never thought of us fitting into the grand scheme of things in E Company. But then it turns out to be the right one.

Or, the client comes to the table with a buyer in mind. "That almost never works," says Krier. "Many times, a client has told me, 'Here's the buyer for you. This is going to be easy for you!' They always give us a buyer or two that they're either talking to, or they want to talk to. And of all the deals we've done over the years, only twice have we ever sold the business to someone that our client said it was going to be this party. When someone just knocks on the door and says, I want to buy your business, the likelihood of that happening is slim to none. And if it does happen, the deals are probably not in the seller's favor."

At Woodbridge, we do the opposite. Our auction-like process drives many more options for you by marketing your company to tens of thousands of strategic businesses. We market to a wide range of potential buyers, which brings more buyers to the table. Seventy-five percent of the time, the buyer turns out to be someone the seller would not have thought of.

Conversely, recalls Krier, "I had a prospect say to me, the reason why I'm hiring you is because about 18 years ago, I sold a business. I had an earn-out deal based on performance for $6 million that was tied to EBITDA and I never got a single dollar of that. So he got the cash at closing and never saw a nickel of that $6 million. He said, I made a big mistake and I never want that to happen again. That's why I'm talking with you.' We created a strong auction for him and got him an all cash deal."

Lesson 24: Stick to the timeline

Our mantra here at Woodbridge is, 'Time kills all deals.' So as part of our auction-like process, there's a bid due date. That keeps everyone on their toes and creating an incentive to put in the best possible bids. We also work within a maximum 150-day timeline for the entire sale.

This 150-day time frame is another innovative way we keep everything moving, but it didn't come naturally. It was a learning process. We learned over time that the longer the deal time frame stretches out, the more it puts a deal in jeopardy. So we have spent considerable time trying to condense various parts of the process down to make them more efficient. Now, once we get the letter of intent, we like to close in 45 to 60 days. It's easy to get lost in things that aren't at the heart or the purpose of the transaction. So a tight schedule keeps everyone on track.

Our most recent win in this area: Between 2021 and 2022, we shaved a week off of prep time, providing faster turnaround of client documents and getting deals in the market faster.

Beware: A buyer can continually ask for more information to try to delay a deal until it is more favorable for them. Also, the company's performance can suddenly suffer a downward inflection due to economic events that have nothing to do with the company but causes buyers to get skittish. So it's really important to keep things moving at a quick pace. You have to recognize when it's time to tell a buyer to stop their additional requests and close the deal.

We had a transaction with a company on the west coast that was due to close on a Friday. The lawyers decided to wrap it up on Monday. Then the business had an incident where someone felt mistreated and filed a lawsuit. Needless to say the buyer did not close on Monday. It took a while for press to calm down and for the buyer to see the way through. The deal closed 60 days later but it was touch and go.

Lesson 25: Brush up on how to sell your business

As entrepreneurs, both Don and I have firsthand knowledge and experience of how horrendous it can be for a small business to sell their company. So we work hard to provide solutions to problems before they happen. One of those solutions was the build-out of the management training program we described earlier in this book.

Woodbridge runs these meetings with intensity and total immersion. "Business owners are smart and they may be good at selling their widgets, but they've never sold a business before so they may not know what they're doing," says Bill Perrone, an attorney with law firm William and Dana LLP in Stamford, Connecticut, which has represented sellers in some of Woodbridge's transactions. "In these management meetings, Woodbridge teaches business owners how to talk to prospective buyers and provide the right answers."

Management training also helps sellers learn about what buyers are looking for. Our methodologies are very structured. We have people show up, pay attention, be interactive, and become wedded to our timetable. We keep everyone marching along at a brisk pace, because anything can happen at any time.

Lesson 26: Create a TED Talk about your company

Two years ago, Woodbridge added TED Talks to their management training program. Here, the seller creates and practices presenting a 6- to 6-1/2-minute video designed to drive thought-provoking questions from the buyer. It's a conceptual overview of their business—a series of headlines if you will; this gives the buyer a sense of the whole business and stimulates pointed follow-up questions. This is in addition to a company video. Both are played at the beginning of every meeting with a buyer.

Perrone calls the TED Talk idea brilliant. "As they say, a picture's worth 1,000 words. When you take a short video, usually you're in your element, such as on the shop floor, and it brings your company and your people to life. So your buyer says, 'That company is interesting, those people are interesting and, I'd like to work with them.' You can't get that from a confidential information memorandum where you're reading words and numbers on a page."

Every buyer wants to know everything you know about your business. They want to be you and they want to get in your head and do their best to learn everything you know because you've been living and breathing the business. So their lawyers and accountants are going to poke around and do what's called a quality of earnings analysis.

But Woodbridge's closers are very good at moving the process along. We recently closed a deal in 21 days from signing the letter of intent. So keep your eye on the prize, because you started this process to exit. And the time goes very quickly.

Krier always tells prospects, "If you've been through a dress rehearsal, then you know exactly what you're going to say when you sit in front of a buyer and have a conversation. That's what the TED Talks are for. You're not going to spend 30 minutes talking about your golf game. You're going to be focused on telling the story about your business, where it can go, and what the opportunities are for the future. That's because we coach sellers on what a buyer needs to know and understand about their business to buy it."

You only get to sell your business once, so if you're thinking about selling your business, now would be a good time to make a move. "There's $1 trillion in private equity money waiting to be deployed," says Perrone, "and the people who run those funds will likely have potential buyers for a wide variety of businesses."

Your buyer is out there. Now is the time to connect with them.

Key Lessons Learned:

- *Think outside the box when it comes to who may buy your business*

- *Practice telling the story of your business on video*

- *Stick to the timeline*

WOODBRIDGE
International

1764 Litchfield Turnpike | Suite 250 | New Haven, CT 06525
203.389.8400 | woodbridgegrp.com

Conclusion:
Woodbridge— the Next 30 Years

Robert Koenig
Founder and CEO
Woodbridge International

WOODBRIDGE
International
Mergers & Acquisitions Since 1993

In this book, we've given you 30 years of evolution, knowledge, and wisdom. But we are students of the business and are constantly thinking about how to make systems and processes better, how to streamline things, and how to speed things up. We're constantly learning.

Now, what will you do with this information? Do you want to lead your company into the next 30 years or sell it tomorrow? Either way, we are ready for you whenever you are ready.

Twenty-five percent of companies make it through the first 10 years. And we're at 30. Every year, about 15,000 companies change hands. Our market is 250,000 companies. Thirty years from now will that market be 1 million companies? 2 million? 5 million? We see an amazing future ahead.

30 years built on trust

Trust is a massive driver of our business. Our clients trust us because they're putting their largest asset in our hands. And we're able to give them advice because we're coming from a good place—because we understand what they're going through and how big a decision this is.

Take George, for instance. He was hesitating to sell his business because he didn't need the money. Years ago, it was worth

$2 million, but now he's going to get $30 million because he's finally doing well. Why was it a good time to sell? Because the business was profitable and the trends were positive. He wanted to hold off and I had to look him in the eye and say, "This is the best deal you're ever going to get." And he went with it. That's trust.

We're not in an easy business, because we're dealing with emotion. We're dealing with irrational behavior. But we know what we're doing, because we've been living and breathing this for 30 years. When it's the right time we know—we can see it. So trust our experience, our wisdom, and our gut.

We're obsessed over this business and I think most of our clients are obsessed over their businesses too, but they get to the point where they're burned out, because running a business can burn a person out. But know that we've got you. Trust comes from who we are—from our wisdom and experience. Once we have trust, then we can be honest, direct, give advice, and give counsel, because that person has hired us to do a job, and that is to sell their business.

The world is your oyster

As a business owner, you, like us, have a future full of unlimited opportunities where anything is possible. You have the ability to make change, to bring your unique skill set to your company and to produce and innovate. If you stay true to your core beliefs and continue to be open-minded and in continual learning mode, you can build a legacy—a great company that lasts long after you've passed the torch.

At Woodbridge, our brand is our team and our culture. We believe that none of us is as smart as all of us. Together, we believe our brand will become a household name in the middle market.

What we as business owners do can change. And how we do it can change. But our core beliefs and philosophy should never change. Being truthful, honest, transparent, humble, giving credit, working hard, having grit, determination, thoughtfulness, passion and creativity…leading by example and loving what we do. These are what define us and should be what defines you.

Remember, the past is your lesson, the present is your gift, and the future is your motivation. Here's to 30 more years!

Notes: